Your Children Can Change the World!

How homeschoolers can prepare their children for leadership in society, in business, and in government

by Ginny Seuffert

Your Children Can Change the World!

How homeschoolers can prepare their children for leadership in society, in business, and in government

by Ginny Seuffert

Copyright © 2016 Seton Home Study School

All rights reserved. No part of this book may be reproduced without written permission of the publisher, except by a reviewer who may quote brief passages in a review.

Printed in the United States of America.

ISBN: 978-1-60704-900-5

Published by Seton Press.
Visit us on the Web at http://www.setonbooks.com/

SETON PRESS
1350 Progress Drive
Front Royal, VA 22630

Contents

Foreword	v
Introduction	1
The First Theme: **Develop a Theory of Human Nature from Studying the Liberal Arts**	7
The Second Theme: **Develop Strong Skills in the Active Literacies**	13
The Third Theme: **Gain Insight into Major Institutional Forms Including Courts, Corporations, Military, and Education**	19
The Fourth Theme: **Repeated Exercises in the Forms of Good Manners and Politeness**	25
The Fifth Theme: **Mental Independence: Why Students Must Start Thinking for Themselves**	32
The Sixth Theme: **Energetic Physical Sports Are not a Luxury**	38

The Seventh Theme:
**Develop a Complete Theory
of Access to Any Workplace**   45

The Eighth Theme:
**Proven Ways to Teach
Your Kids Responsibility**   51

The Ninth Theme:
**Arrive at a Personal
Code of Standards**   56

The Tenth Theme:
**Ways Your Child Can Become
Familiar with the Fine Arts**   62

The Eleventh Theme:
**Stimulate the Power of Accurate
Observation and Recording**   68

The Twelfth Theme:
**The Ability to Deal with
Challenges of All Sorts**   73

The Thirteenth Theme:
**Develop a Habit of Caution
in Reasoning to Conclusion**   79

The Fourteenth Theme:
**How to Develop (& Test)
Judgment in Children**   85

Conclusion   89

Foreword

Education by Injunction or Aspiration?

by John Taylor Gatto

1.

A wise philosopher who served as a policeman in Alaska once said "Nobody can 'give' you an education. Only a schooling can be given; an education must be taken."

When the transit of European culture came to the wild lands of North America, two highly contradictory outlooks on the training of young people came with it: the exceedingly severe Christianity of John Calvin which taught that children were not to be trusted to incline toward positive outcomes and were as tainted by the Original Sin of disobedience as older men and women; but this outlook, embedded in Calvin's influential classic, *Institutes of the Christian Religion*, the foundation of Britain's official state religion of Anglicanism, was accompanied by a diametrically opposite point of view transmitted by the independent and dissenting religions (Presbyterian, Congregational, Quaker, Baptist, et. al.), a point of view originating in the Old Norse culture of Viking Scandinavia that the young should be trained to add value to the general community and be thought of as full citizens with full obligations.

The Calvinist mistrust of the young became the guiding philosophy of a new secular institution in world history—mass forced training of the young under direction of employees of the political state; while the "Viking Mind" philosophy of equality and full responsibility became the guiding philosophy of elite private boarding schooling training at schools like Groton, St.Paul's. Milton Academy, Choate, Exeter, Andover, and the like, which, over time, statistically produced an impressively large fraction of America's leaders in politics, business, science, and the arts.

2.

As a public school teacher, a number of my colleagues, friends, and students' parents were graduates of elite private boarding schools and, in time, that awakened my curiosity about the differences in curriculum between those widely praised institutions which charged $50,000 a year and the much-despised institution for which I worked. One friend, a graduate of Lawrenceville, a feeder prep school for Princeton, told me that one clear way to understand the difference was to think about the continual rhetorical boast of government school advocates that they helped students get "a good job," while "jobs" in general—as a category—were held in contempt by founders and clientele of the best proprietary schools because they meant a lifetime of obedience to some total stranger's whims—not a fitting goal for a free man or woman. Private schooling, at its best, intended for its clientele to discover a way to earn money by "adding value" to the world at large by developing particular God-given talents and exchanging these for income.

Such outcomes were unlikely under a regime of injunction-driven (excessively rule-driven) pedagogy because that left no time and energy to learn to aspire to better things, to participate fully in taking an education for oneself, a process that demanded very extensive real world experience which school confinement precluded; demanded also that education-seekers select their own goals to an extent, and learn to be their own judges—behaviors no tightly-layered bureaucracy can tolerate. Elite education aims to produce bosses and leaders, not followers and employees, my friend said. You can't do that in a public school because the supervisors won't allow it! Public schools have a different function in a mass-production commercial economy, an essential one: their students must learn to consume things, uncritically as possible, as often as possible, both products, services, and expert opinions—we ask public employees who teach to discourage initiative and imagination in the masses because a stable social order only has room on it's pyramid of privileges for a limited number of winners on the upper levels, and needs most to occupy lower positions near the base. When too many are allowed to aspire instead of following injunctions, dangerous social conditions occur, as they did in Germany after World War I, a nation heavily laden with college graduates beyond the number that its economy could absorb. The ambitions of the educated produced a spectacular inflation in which a single postage stamp or a ham sandwich cost a wheel barrow full of money to purchase—an example well-understood by political leaders.

3.

Despite possessing an understanding of why the numbers of truly educated men and women must be limited in a healthy society, I decided in my first years of teaching to introduce elite private school curriculum into my 8th grade classes of (mostly) lower economic class kids, discarding the inferior curriculum mandated by the city's top educational authorities. After intensely researching the top 20 or so elite boarding schools, examining their materials, interviewing their graduates, using library resources where available, visiting campuses on weekends by automobile, I was able to identify some fourteen principles followed in all of the top 20 that had no analogues in public schools. I shall not list them here for Mrs. Seuffert's book, which you hold, does that admirably. Suffice it to say that translating these principles into lessons and actions for my 8th graders revolutionized my classes, my students' lives, their self-images soared, opportunities opened up quite dramatically for them in scholarships and prizes, employment, and a measure of local fame as they performed services for the influential West Side neighborhood of Manhattan which surprised and shocked (pleasantly) older people who thought children of that age and social class were incapable of aspiring sufficiently to manage their own educational progress.

4.

In her book *Your Children Can Change the World*, Mrs. Seuffert has offered the rest of us a transformation of the 14 principles I discovered into a priceless toolkit of ideas how anyone responsible for the education of others can strive to achieve the same value for their student(s) as a wealthy kid would receive if his/her parents sent them to Episcopal High (which Sen. John McCain attended) or to Andover (which both President Bushes did). Following Mrs. Seuffert's advice, your students will seek the same skills that history has shown leaders possess in business, politics, arts and sciences—rather than the trivializing grade and gold-star chasing, relevant to nothing significant, that public schools or common garden-variety private ones pursue as evidences of learning. Wake up! Those prizes have no lasting value, connect to nothing useful in later life, while competence in "the active literacies," one of the 14 categories Mrs. Seuffert develops, will serve you faithfully for the balance of your days, and may easily become the basis of a comfortable livelihood and high reputation.

The author has a unique qualification that impresses me beyond words: she is mother to 12 children and grandmother to 21, so she has directly or indirectly produced 33 human beings—an accomplishment which, to me, testifies to an unusual talent for assuming responsibility that shines through this very worthwhile book, which is certain to grace your homeschooling experience if you use it faithfully to fashion a $50,000 education for your daughters and sons.

x

Introduction

Independent study, community service, adventures and experience, large doses of privacy and solitude, a thousand different apprenticeships, the one-day variety or longer – these are all powerful, cheap and effective ways to start a real reform of schooling. But no large-scale reform is ever going to work to repair our damaged children and our damaged society until we force open the idea of "school" to include family as the main engine of education. If we use schooling to break children away from parents — and make no mistake, that has been the central function of schools since John Cotton announced it as the purpose of the Bay Colony schools in 1650 and Horace Mann announced it as the purpose of Massachusetts schools in 1850 — we're going to continue to have the horror show we have right now.

John Taylor Gatto

When I began homeschooling my children in the late 1980's, the question I was most often asked was, "Is that legal?" With the popularity of home education exploding, I have not heard that question in years, but confusion still remains. Will children who never enter a classroom learn how to socialize with others, or are they doomed to be quirky, or worse yet, weird? How can a home environment provide athletics and team sports? Will homeschooled kids be denied enrichment of exposure to music and the fine arts? How can they possibly learn upper level math and science, or a foreign language? Many parents worry that homeschooled children will be at a disadvantage when applying for college, or in obtaining scholarships to pay for college. In fact, I have been asked more than once if students graduating from school at home can even *attend* college.

Of course, they can and do. Many colleges and universities are so happy with home-educated students that they actively, even aggressively, recruit them. Far from being unsocialized, research indicates that homeschooled students are less likely to abuse drugs, get involved in premature sexual activity, suffer depression, or get arrested. Most of the time, they make the challenging transition from home life to dorm life with fewer problems than their peers who graduate from brick and mortar schools. Frequently, child professionals in the arts and top athletes receive their education outside of a classroom. Taken as a group, home schoolers outperform more traditionally educated students in virtually every area of endeavor.

Now one top educator is suggesting a path home educated students can follow in order to assume leadership positions in business, politics and the professions, including education, medicine and law.

Master educator John Taylor Gatto was named New York City Teacher of the Year in 1989, 1990, and 1991, and New York State Teacher of the Year in 1991. In 1991, in an op-ed piece in the *Wall Street Journal*, Gatto announced he was abandoning the New York City government school system stating that he was no longer willing to "hurt kids to make a living." "Government schooling," Gatto claimed, "kills the family by monopolizing the best times of childhood and by teaching disrespect for home and parents." He has devoted his life since then to articulating a different vision of education that turns children into lifetime learners.

John Taylor Gatto rejects compulsory government education, stating that it confuses students, making them indifferent, as well as emotionally and intellectually dependent. Children schooled in brick and mortar schools are in constantly supervised situations, with little free time to explore their environment and develop personal interests and talents, and are actively prevented from maturing into independent thinkers and doers. In public school, they are programmed to seek constant affirmation — gold stars and high grades — for their self-esteem instead of gaining confidence by acquiring new skills and achieving their own objectives.

Some time ago, Gatto examined the curricula taught in our nation's most successful private prep schools, where the wealthy and powerful groom their children to assume positions of leadership in government, industry and the professions. These institutions are quite different from government schools, and although each employs a different philosophy and curriculum, Gatto identified **fourteen themes that they hold in common**. As I reviewed these themes, it struck me that Catholic homeschoolers are in a unique position to inculcate these characteristics into our own school day.

But why should we?

It is no coincidence that a substantial number of American leaders, in every field of endeavor, hail from wealthy and influential families. These families have the financial resources to ensure that their children get the best possible academic and personal formation, enabling them to follow previous generations into positions of power and authority. Of course, parents from less-entitled backgrounds sometimes do not share these high aspirations for their children. Placing less value on worldly attainment, faithful Catholic families are often more concerned that their children will become adults who obey the Ten Commandments, enter religious life or raise strong families, and live up to their personal commitments. Most of us regard impeccable character to be the most essential objective of child rearing.

Strangely enough, men and women of noble character are just the category of individuals American society so desperately needs to assume leadership in local communities and at a national level, in our parishes, government agencies, and businesses, and to represent the United States on the international stage. Our nation – indeed our world – desperately needs leaders committed to the highest levels of integrity and virtue.

As Mr. Gatto makes clear in his foreword, top private schools such as Exeter or Andover consciously go about the business of preparing their students to lead the world. Government schools, educating about ninety-percent of the population, do not. As these top private institutions educate a fraction of one percent of the nation's youth, the system seems to make sense. After all, not everyone will lead.

At any given time in the United States, there is one President and 300 million people who aren't President. There are 9 Supreme Court Justices and 300 million people who aren't Supreme Court Justices. There are 538 members of Congress and 300 million people who aren't members of Congress.

The people who hold leadership positions in the United States are not random. They are people who were groomed for leadership through their education. President Obama graduated from Columbia University and Harvard Law School. Every single current justice of the Supreme Court graduated from Harvard, Yale, or Columbia Law School. The top three alma maters of members of Congress are Harvard, Yale, and Stanford. This should not deter us; rather, it should spur us on. The citizen statesman founded the United States and the self-made man built our industries. Well-formed Catholic children from less-entitled backgrounds can be consciously prepared for influential positions, as well.

Future leaders need to be rigorously and thoroughly prepared. Sky-high tuition at top private prep schools places these institutions out of reach of the average American household, but home education is incredibly affordable. We homeschooling parents have a unique opportunity to teach our children not only the doctrines of our Faith, but also the extraordinary level of accomplishment of Catholics who preceded us. Because home educated students do not waste time on school buses, lining up in corridors, and sitting through assemblies, they have more time to study dance, practice musical instruments, dissect an earthworm, stroll through botanical gardens, or join a debate club. Catholic home education can be the equivalent of a high-end prep school education, at a tiny fraction of the price. Let's make the most of it.

To Be Clear

These fourteen themes of private prep schools belong entirely to John Taylor Gatto. The idea of applying them to Catholic homeschooling to produce leaders from our ranks belongs entirely to me. His writings often focus on the bleak failure of government schools. This book concentrates on the hope represented by families teaching their own children in their homes and communities. My approach to these themes is, I hope, thoroughly and faithfully Catholic.

The First Theme

Develop a Theory of Human Nature from Studying the Liberal Arts

Whatever an education is, it should make you a unique individual, not a conformist; it should furnish you with an original spirit with which to tackle the big challenges; it should allow you to find values which will be your road map through life; it should make you spiritually rich, a person who loves whatever you are doing, wherever you are, whomever you are with; it should teach you what is important, how to live and how to die.

John Taylor Gatto

John Taylor Gatto's first theme is that students must develop a **"theory of human nature as embodied in history, philosophy, theology, literature and law."** If Catholic graduates will be assuming positions of influence, they must understand what provokes others to act the way they do, and how these individuals can be motivated to think and act differently. This theme should be natural for Catholic homeschooling families, who follow in the liberal arts tradition of the great medieval Western universities and base their theory of human nature on the teachings of Holy Mother Church.

To Catholics, human beings are creatures made in the image and likeness of God, who exist to know, love and serve God and one another in this world and to be happy with Him in the next. This philosophy will not only help students develop a personal code of conduct, but also give them a firm grasp of the motivations and actions of others. Our goal must be to deepen our students' understanding of the Christian view of humanity through the agencies that Mr. Gatto suggests: theology, history, philosophy, literature and law.

Theology

While our religion (theology) classes must inculcate virtuous habits and pious practices, they must also awaken our students' interest in how God revealed Himself and His Divine Plan, first to His Chosen People, the Israelites, and then through the teachings of His Son, Jesus Christ. The teaching authority of the Catholic Church, the *magisterium*, explains these teachings in our own day. Their personal relationship to their Creator often determines the caliber of citizen, spouse, parent, and worker that children will become.

Theology also teaches students their responsibility to their fellow humans. They themselves have a personal obligation to feed the hungry and give drink to the thirsty; clothe the naked and give shelter to the homeless. They must care for the sick, ransom the captive, and bury the dead, as Christians before them have done. Sometimes, Catholics perform these services through taxes they pay to the government, or contributions they make to charitable organizations, but these do not satisfy their responsibility. Students must develop habits of personal giving of their own time, talent and money, and help to advance a society where others generously share in these tasks.

Government schools abandoned teaching Judeo-Christian ethics decades ago. Homeschooling parents have a unique and unrepeatable opportunity to use Faith studies as a means to develop ideas of how human beings should interact with one another.

History

George Santayana famously said, "Those who do not learn history are doomed to repeat it." Studying how historical figures have respected and protected the inherent dignity of others, or failed to do so, gives a unique understanding of what motivates human behavior in our own time. Examples abound.

In the Roman Empire, the common citizen developed indifference to republican ideals as the government doled out free grain and entertainment to them. "Bread and circuses" became the surest way to buy the vote to get and keep power. Ask your students to consider if our American obsession with entertainment and sports figures, coupled with social welfare entitlement programs, are a modern version of "bread and circuses"?

As I write this, a socialist is seeking the nomination for president. Have your children learned about Socialism? Is it a good idea? Where has it worked, or has it worked at all?

Students need to understand these questions, and thousands more like them, and diligently research to seek answers to them. How can citizens possibly make intelligent decisions about the future, if they lack understanding of the past?

Philosophy

Philosophy deals with the problems humanity faces as it struggles to grasp the reality of existence, reason, and knowledge.

A practical example of this theme is found when our students study a document such as *The Declaration of Independence*. In the very first paragraph, Jefferson states that the residents of the colonies are entitled to a "separate and equal station" by the "Laws of Nature and of Nature's God," and claims that their fundamental rights are "inalienable" because they receive them not from a benign or even benevolent government, but directly from their Creator.

Ask your students to go even deeper. When Jefferson speaks of Nature and Nature's God, does he mean two different systems of origin for human rights, or is he claiming that the two systems — the laws of God and the laws of nature — exist in harmony as one? Carefully considered, this document is worthy of study for more than its historical or legal significance; it reveals essential aspects of the human condition.

Literature

Great fiction will accomplish the same purpose. By reading great works that have stood the test of time, students gain insight into what motivates human thoughts and actions. Sometimes these are virtues such as courage, loyalty, honesty, as well as faith in God and charity towards neighbor. Other times, human actions can be attributed to avarice, concupiscence, materialism, and disordered ambition. Hesitation or lack of action can be the result of indolence or despair.

These virtues and vices, and many more, are the heart of great story telling. Readers mourn alongside Meg, Jo, and Amy when Beth dies, and learn about the essential role families play in overcoming heartache. They ride on a raft down the Mississippi with Huck and Jim, all the while studying racism, drunkenness, and hypocrisy, and at the same time loyalty and willingness to defy societal norms to do the right thing.

Homeschooled students will be better persons for witnessing Sydney Carton's serenity as he waits to climb the scaffold to his heroic death, tenderly comforting a condemned seamstress. Desperate, grinding poverty becomes real to them when Fantine prostitutes herself to care for her child. Most will never face choices like Thomas More who can only save his life by compromising with an evil law, or Jean Valjean who will remain free if he allows an innocent man to be sent to the galleys, or Jane Eyre who must abandon her only hope of happiness to retain her virtue, but something about how they make their decisions gives young readers important insights into human nature.

Law

Issues of the rule of law dominate much of our nation's conversation today. Older students will be familiar with the recent Supreme Court decision legalizing marriage between persons of the same gender. Many Americans rejoiced because they were happy with the outcome, but we should consider Justice Scalia's ominous dissent. "This practice of constitutional revision by an unelected committee of nine, always accompanied (as it is today) by extravagant praise of liberty, robs the People of the most important liberty they asserted in the Declaration of Independence and won in the Revolution of 1776: the freedom to govern themselves."

Similar warnings were sounded in 1973 when the Supreme Court legalized abortion on demand, citing a right to privacy not found in the Constitution, but rather in the "penumbras" formed by "emanations" in the Bill of Rights. These are both profound issues affecting the family, the foundational cell of society. In coming years, leaders will need to address questions regarding the United States Constitution, the rule of law, and the place of the ordinary citizen in relation to them. Students must have a strong grasp of our nation's foundational documents to tackle these issues.

The next time your students grumble about memorizing the catechism, studying for a history quiz, turning off the TV and reading a book, writing a book analysis, or reading a newspaper, remind them that they are being prepared for greatness.

The Second Theme

Develop Strong Skills in the Active Literacies

Active literacies would involve the higher levels of reading, where you're actually entering someone else's mind and feeling the way it moves around an idea, but mainly writing and speaking, because writing and speaking gives access to people, whereas reading's a solitary thing.

John Taylor Gatto

John Taylor Gatto observes that graduates of the successful private prep schools, those destined to assume positions of authority, **have strong experience with the active literacies: writing and public speaking.** It only makes sense. Although reading can enlighten, it is a passive discipline with information only flowing one way. It is by definition a solitary activity, influencing the reader only. The active literacies allow ideas to be formulated and then passed on to others through the spoken or written word. They are key to exerting influence.

Better Writing

Students must have strong backgrounds in composition, able to clearly and forcefully express themselves in the written word. The best way to teach your child how to write is to make sure he or she receives rigorous training and practice in grammar and composition. These subjects must be taught every year in a planned and orderly fashion, but in my experience composition is the last assignment parents and students tackle. I understand why. Composition is multi-disciplinary, requiring students to gather and organize their thoughts, and then write them down using good penmanship (or keyboarding), remembering proper grammar, capitalization and punctuation. These are not assignments that work well with the numerous distractions in many homes. Nevertheless, strong composition skills are so essential to success in college and later life that we must persevere.

John Gatto wisely suggests daily practice—there is simply no substitute for that. Here are a few ideas parents might remember as they assign some writing each day:

- Do not allow your students to use weak, generic words. Insist that they specify what they mean; for example squirrels do not "move"; they scamper, and snakes slither. There are not lots of "things" in our yard; there are flowers, patio furniture, and a swing set.
- Encourage the children to use vivid words to describe. As an assignment, have them write sentences using variations of common words, for example "big" could be sizeable, huge, giant, enormous, and immense. Write each word in a correct sentence.
- For younger children, provide a "word box" to give them ideas.
- Let your children learn how to keyboard as early as possible. Seton Home Study School has noticed that work done on a computer generally scores a higher grade than handwritten assignments—perhaps

because students give more complete answers. It is certainly much easier to edit and polish a composition when using a computer.
- Show students how to locate synonyms and definitions on the word processor. Provide a dictionary and thesaurus for kids using pen and paper.
- Some children really struggle with composition. Do not hesitate to help with organization and ideas. Start with the easiest compositions such as descriptive or instructional paragraphs: "describe your bedroom", or "how do you make a peanut butter and jelly sandwich?"
- Assign different genres of writing: describe various scenes, narrate an event or series of events, express an opinion and give reasons to support your opinion, or provide instructions.
- Good reading leads to good writing. Set aside some time everyday for your children to read. High quality literature is best, but allowing children to follow their interests often leads to a tremendous expansion of those interests. If your kids are interested in insects, let them read and write about that.

Remember, students must write every day, even if it is just a short journal recording the weather and events or plans of the day. When they do, parents will see real improvement over time.

Social Correspondence

Encourage your children to write to family members and friends. Make sure they send thank you notes for all gifts and hospitality. Grandparents, godparents, and aunts and uncles will love to get chatty newsletters. Forgo pre-printed invitations, and assign your children to send letters asking others to join your family for special occasions. Allow younger children to illustrate their writing. Delight your friends and relatives.

Public Speaking

The ability to express oneself in the spoken word can be every bit as important as being able to write well. Finding opportunities for public speaking can be more of a challenge — but not impossible — to find. Here are some ideas:

- Read aloud a poem from the *Faith and Freedom* readers to Dad at night or grandparents when they visit.
- Memorize a short poem, speech, or reading each week and recite it for each other during class, or for company at Sunday dinner.
- See if your church is looking for young lectors, or religious education teachers or assistants.
- Suggest to your homeschool support group that one or two meetings each year be dedicated to highlighting schoolwork, instead of social or field trip activities. Let students prepare a short exhibition, and explain their work to the group.

- Your homeschool support group can encourage a debate club.
- Encourage students to become involved in local causes. If your child is in favor of the new town pool, help him or her prepare and practice a short speech to give at a public meeting.

Remember to remind children to stand straight and use their best diction. If they will be speaking outside the home, insist on proper attire. Children will also gain confidence in public settings if they participate in instrumental music recitals, theatre groups, dance recitals, or even sports teams where they must "perform" for strangers.

Start in the Family

Finally, the earliest exercises in public speaking involve good manners. Teach your children how to address strangers by shaking hands and answering questions politely. Ask them to introduce their friends to you. Do not let them hide behind a curtain of shyness. Never allow your children to hide behind video game screens during meals, in company, or in public. Eat meals together and discuss the events of the day. Constant practice can make difficult or uncomfortable experiences become a matter of course.

In our household, five children, all younger than ten years old, participate in dinnertime conversation. They each take a turn listing three things they are grateful for, and then must give the name of one person in whom they "saw God" today. It is refreshing to hear a six-year-old say how thankful she is "for this delicious dinner," because she played with her friends, and because her Grandpa took her for an ice cream treat. She "saw God" in her brother when he walked her to her friend's house.

Teaching children to express their ideas on paper or in person provides them with an invaluable skill for future success.

The Third Theme

Gain Insight into Major Institutional Forms Including Courts, Corporations, Military, and Education

Children allowed to take responsibility and given a serious part in the larger world are always superior to those merely permitted to play and be passive.

John Taylor Gatto

John Taylor Gatto's Third Theme is that students in prestigious prep schools must **gain insight into major institutional forms including courts, military, and corporations, as well as the ideas that drive them.** By truly understanding these institutions, students mature into responsible citizens who will not be persuaded by opinion-makers in the major media, but will be capable of forming intelligent, independent judgments, and then acting on them. Clearly, to accomplish this, we must emphasize history (especially American), civics and geography in our homeschools, but here are a few other ideas.

Government

Bring your children to your state capital to watch a legislative session, especially one that involves an important issue such as our ability to homeschool free from government intervention. Attend a pro-life rally with your students and listen to the speakers. Watch presidential debates on television. C-Span offers a number of opportunities to watch government bodies go about their work.

On a local level, you might bring your children to town hall or county supervisor meetings, or meetings of the library or school boards. In addition to informing them about community issues, they will learn about rules of order and how responsible citizenship works. Bring your children with you when you vote, and explain the process to them. Discuss the pros and cons of each candidate. Work the polls with teenage students.

Military

If you have a military base or military school nearby, call and find out if they have any events scheduled that are open to the public. Many bases have parades or training graduations. Ask veterans you know to talk to your children about their experiences.

Everyone with Internet access can get a glimpse into duty, honor, and country. The website for Arlington Cemetery gives a beautiful explanation of the Changing of the Guard at the Tomb of the Unknown. It explains how the 3rd U.S. Infantry Regiment, the "Old Guard" is the longest serving active-duty infantry unit in the United States Army, serving since 1784. Another website tours the American Cemetery in Normandy, France, final resting place of our soldiers lost in the D-Day Invasion. Other websites to look at include those of the service academies. See what events are open to the public.

Twelve kids and I can count on one hand the number of times we went to amusement parks. However, I do not have enough fingers and toes to count all the battlefields we have visited. Most of them are free to visit or nearly so, and really bring military history alive. Some historical fiction, and even a number of movies, help children to understand how our fighting forces operate.

Introduce your children to the fine traditions of honor and service found in the United States military.

Business

"Bring Your Child to Work Day" can take on special meaning for homeschooling families as our children have more availability than others. If you cannot bring children to your place of business (or someone else's), make sure you talk about the type of work you do, hours you work, office rules, payroll, taxes—the list goes on and on. When you are in other business establishments, make sure you include your children in the conversation so that they know the nature of the business and the services it provides.

While it is not necessary to share details of your particular situation, talk to your children about family finances in a general way. Make sure they understand what a mortgage is, utility bills, debt, banking, and budgeting, why we need insurance, and for what. Explain that your household finances are a microcosm of how corporations and the government must, or at least should, balance income and expenditures.

Perhaps the best way to teach your children about business is to allow them to do real work. When I was thirteen years old and my brothers were ten and twelve, my dad quit his white-collar job in Manhattan and opened a gas station and repair shop. As with any new business, money was tight for the first few years. My father learned how to do the bookwork for the station, and then taught me, so he could devote his time to earning money, not keeping books. At thirteen, I could keep daily and monthly records of income and expenses, submit credit card charges, and make bank deposits.

In those days, people did not pump their own gas. Stations hired an entry-level "gas jockey" to fuel cars. To save on that expense, my brothers worked when they were not in school. My dad didn't pay them, saying, "If you want to make some money, check customers' oil and wash their windshields. Maybe they'll tip you." And they did.

We had very generous parents; nevertheless, before we reached high school, all my parent's children earned our own spending money, and paid for many of our own expenses. I paid my last two years of Catholic high school tuition out of my own earnings. By the time we graduated, there was no doubt in any of our minds that we could support ourselves one way or another. We paid for our own post-secondary education, and even paid our mom rent.

How times have changed! My dad might be arrested now for giving his kids the gifts of responsibility and hard work.

Education

Do your children know why you homeschool? Do they understand concepts that guide compulsory government education? Are they familiar with national standards that seek to turn out cookie cutter kids who will work and vote as they have been told. Let students know that homeschooling was not some random decision you made to keep them away from bad influences or provide them with an academically superior formation. Write down your reasons for homeschooling in an orderly list and share the list with your children. Assign them a research paper that deals with educational choice, or other related topics. Between themselves and their future children, they will be dealing with educational institutions for much of their lives. Let them understand the forces that drive American education.[1]

Understand the Church

Gatto does not include this final institution, but I believe we should give our homeschooled children a real knowledge of the inner workings of the Catholic Church. Our religion classes teach doctrine, but we also want our children to understand the history and structure of the Roman Catholic Church. Seton Home Study School publishes a book intended for 8th grade religion students entitled *Witness to the Faith*. This book gives the history of the Church, its triumph over persecution, the stories of great saints, and how the Church evolved into its present institutional form.

Understanding the institutional Church can be quite important in our own time. Often homeschooling parents do not understand their rights and their obligations under Church law regarding the education of their children.

---

[1] John Taylor Gatto has written several books and articles that deal with both the history of education in the United States and its status at the beginning of the new millennium. I cannot recommend them highly enough to any parent who wants an insider's look into government schooling.

Seton Educational Media carries a book, *Responsibilities and Rights of Parents in Religious Education*, which spells out both in simple, easy to understand language. This practical guide addresses lots of issues important to Catholic families.

News reports offer another opportunity to show how the Church changes over time as exemplified by the *ordinariates* allowing Anglican Catholics in the United Kingdom, North America and Australia to enter into full communion with Rome while retaining some of their own traditions. If recent history is any indicator, some of your homeschooled children will enter the priesthood and religious life, and have a bit of influence over the institutional Church's future course. Get them ready now.

Public school teachers and college professors report that many teens and young adults are pretty clueless regarding basic institutions of American society. A practical example of this is credit card companies that prey on college students, encouraging them to "establish credit" and then chase their parents when the kids accumulate charges they cannot possibly hope to pay. As they become adult citizens, your children will benefit from insight into our government, military, financial and religious institutions.

Society will benefit from the contributions of well-formed Americans who possess thoughtful understanding of the foundations that guide it.

The Fourth Theme

Repeated Exercises in the Forms of Good Manners and Politeness

School is a twelve-year jail sentence where bad habits are the only curriculum truly learned. I teach school and win awards doing it. I should know.

John Taylor Gatto

Gatto's fourth theme is that expensive private schools offer their students **repeated exercises in the practice of good manners and courtesy** based on the "utter truth that politeness and civility are the foundations of all future relationships and the key of access to places a person might want to go." Interestingly Gatto, who taught in government schools for decades, notes that "Public schools are laboratories of rudeness and cruelty, sloppiness and coarseness," an observation that certainly leaves an opportunity for homeschoolers. My own experience confirms this fourth theme that polite people will go further in life.

Years ago, my eldest son attended a private military academy near our home. Gabe was a day student, but most of his classmates were boarders, so our house became a popular weekend destination. The cadets were not allowed to keep civilian clothes at school so they would arrive at our house in uniform, all the while displaying simply lovely military manners. Every meal brought, "Thank you, Ma'am; that was delicious."

When my husband came home from work, our visitors would immediately hop to their feet, shake his hand, and say, "Thanks for having us, Sir. We appreciate the hospitality."

I recall being charmed at the time, and thinking that this conduct would take them far in life. Since then, I have worked in Human Resources, and can assure you that the job applicant who greets the interviewer with a firm handshake, dresses appropriately, sits straight, speaks politely, and sends a thank you note, certainly has a leg up for the job. Here's what you can do to give your children this advantage.

Practice the Magic Words until they become automatic

As soon as they learn to speak, children should be prompted to add "please" to any request, and say "thank you" for any favor granted. Every family member should politely greet or say farewell to others when they enter or leave a room. Children should be taught to make introductions: "Mom, this is my friend Karen, Karen this is my mom. Everyone calls her Miss Betty." Conversation in your home should be filled with phrases that show concern for others. "Would it be too much trouble?" "Do you mind?" "I'm sorry to be a bother."

Interrupting adult conversation for matters that clearly could have waited until a lull, is a particularly troubling trend in children. Breaking into the middle of another person's sentence should be reserved for emergencies along the lines of a house fire, respiratory arrest, or arterial bleeding. Most other requests can be put on hold. One hint I picked up to teach patience to younger children is to allow them to silently place a hand on mom's. Mom then covers the hand with her own to let the child know she is aware that he is waiting. Then, at her convenience, she asks, "Is there something you wanted?'

Children must learn to say, "I'm sorry for interrupting, Mom, but may I … ? "

These simple courtesies will not only prepare young people for the future, but also make life at home considerably more pleasant right now.

Practice table manners at every meal

In former times, family life centered around meals at the kitchen table. Today, we need to turn off the screens and try to have as many meals together as possible, sitting at a table, allowing children to practice their table manners until they become second nature. Here are some basics:

- Everybody waits for the food server to sit and the family says grace together before anyone starts eating.
- Plates should be passed and anyone old enough to use utensils should use them.
- While no one will every really notice that a person uses a dinner fork to eat salad, everyone must learn how to properly use knives, forks and spoons. I am surprised at the number of educated people who spear their meat vertically with a fork, as if they needed to kill it before they cut it.
- Every family member should thank the cook and offer to help with clean up.

- Express appreciation for a delicious meal, but remember that personal preferences are not appropriate table talk. The only thing to say when presented with a less appetizing selection is "No, thank you."
- It goes without saying that no one should chew with an open mouth or do anything else that might ruin the appetite of others.
- Children should ask to be excused before leaving the table, and adults should excuse themselves.

Learn the Basics of Hospitality

As they get older, teach your children to welcome guests in your home, "It's so nice to see you again, Mrs. Smith. Have a seat and I'll get Mom." Have them offer refreshments, even if it's just a glass of water. Let them learn how to make polite small talk if you will not be available right away.

If you have nothing nice to say, say nothing at all

The best way to teach this particular courtesy is for parents to practice it at every available opportunity. Avoid gossip like the plague that it is. Instruct children to speak nicely about others and do not tolerate name-calling. When my children tattled on others, I would remind them to "Worry about your own thoughts and deeds. That should keep you busy." Sometimes negative talk cannot be avoided entirely due to circumstances, but still can be framed in a way that avoids speaking ill of others. For example, if the children ask about neighbors who are getting divorced, it is not necessary to share details you may know. Instead you can focus on how sad it is when people get divorced and encourage your children to pray for them.

Social media offers special challenges for those who wish to keep a civil tongue. It is remarkable how unpleasant others can get with total strangers on the Internet. Encourage your children to remember the biblical admonition to "turn the other cheek," and not respond in kind to social media offensiveness.

Dress appropriately for the occasion

Americans have turned casual into an art form and this is perhaps most evident in our sloppy attire. When we dress suitably for social occasions, we show respect for those around us. When we dress elegantly for Sunday Mass, we especially show respect for Our Lord in the Blessed Sacrament. At the same time, young people need to learn how to present themselves in the professional world. You would be shocked at the number of job applicants who show up for an interview in jeans, sporting multiple piercings, pastel hair color, or who are simply unkempt. As a former Human Resources professional, I can tell you, such applicants are only hired as a last resort. Encourage your children to dress appropriately and well for all occasions.

Be Polite in Public

Insist that your children greet people they know politely and by name, shake a hand that is offered, and answer any questions in a clear voice. This can be really tough for a shy child, but formal manners are the answer to that problem. It is easy to interact with those we know and love. Courtesy is the tool we use to deal with people we may not know, or perhaps not like very much. Knowing the pleasant thing to say for any occasion helps us deal with awkward situations or if we are somewhat tongue-tied.

Have your children hold the door for elders, and allow others to go first though a door. Have them step aside for an older person on a sidewalk or in a parking lot. Encourage them to offer help to someone who is obviously struggling with a package. Teach them to refer to adults by last name with a title unless requested to do otherwise. Remind them how unacceptably rude it is for young people to play electronics games or text their friends in restaurants or in the company of others.

Teach Children to Handle Tough Moments in Life

Young people, and a surprising number of adults, have no idea how to act or what to say when faced with the reality of death, devastating illness, or other types of family or community crises. It is best to equip our children with the social tools they need to face these uncomfortable circumstances while they are young. Tell them what to say and do.

Take your children to wakes and funerals *before* a close friend or family member dies. If the casket is open, simply tell them that, "Mr. Oldman's body will be in a big box. His soul is gone and is with God now. We will kneel down and say a prayer. When you see Mrs. Oldman, tell her you are sorry Mr. Oldman died, and that you will always remember him for something, such as the funny stories he told you."

If you are dropping off a meal at a sick person's house, bring the children with you. "Let's tell Mrs. Jones how happy we are that her mom is feeling better and ask her if she needs us to do anything else." Shielding children from life's difficult challenges does them no favor. They grow up into adults who may want to do the right thing, but have no idea where to start or what to say.

It's worth the effort

Some of you may consider all of this to be excessively formal and wish to keep your home life more casual, but John Gatto believes — as do I — that the opposite is true. By insisting on civility all the time, fine manners become easygoing and a way of life. Most importantly, courtesy demonstrates an authentic Christian concern for others, and will open up many doors in your children's future. People do not forget kind words and actions.

The Fifth Theme

Mental Independence: Why Students Must Start Thinking for Themselves

In a home school, the kid does 95% of the work. But in a school system, since it's an indoctrination system, a teacher has to do 95% of the work.

In centuries past, the time of childhood and adolescence would have been occupied with real work, real charity, real adventures and the realistic search for real mentors who might teach you what you really want to learn.

John Taylor Gatto

Gatto's fifth theme is that **entitled students are given ample opportunity to work independently.**

Gatto asserts, and my own experience confirms, that government schools charge teachers with filling about 80% to 90% of students' time in class and often send home hours of directed homework. Students are not left alone to mull over and work out their classroom assignments, but increasingly are instructed to collaborate with other students, a process sometimes referred to as peer-directed learning.

Common Core exemplar videos, easily accessed online, show students reciting in unison, and being directed to collaborate and "find consensus" solving math problems. They break up into groups, and then indicate — thumbs up! — when they can all agree on a possible solution.

Teachers congratulate group consensus and then look to establish class consensus. In other words, students are directed not to figure out a math problem on their own, but to actively seek peer approval for individual strategies.

One Common Core standard calls for students to: "Prepare for and participate effectively in a range of conversations and collaborations with diverse partners, building on others' ideas and expressing their own clearly and persuasively." [2] The ability to collaborate, we are told by educators, is key to students' future success working on professional teams and committees. Perhaps this is true for future worker bees, cogs in the industrial wheel, but *leaders* need to be trained to work independently, and that's just what successful private schools do.

Teachers working in Common Core classrooms report that students must justify solutions according to set formulas, and are constantly groomed to spit out certain answers for standardized tests.[3] There is virtually no time for researching topics from different angles or approaches. Rarely are children allowed to explore solutions, perhaps fail, learn from failure, and gain personal mastery.

In the not too distant past, children needed to think for themselves

In former times, many working class kids learned to think and work independently when their labor was required on the family farm or in the family business. In

[2] http://www.corestandards.org/ELA-Literacy/CCRA/SL/1/
[3] As I write this, irate parents are posting a Common Core math assignment on social media. A child was assigned to use a "repeated addition strategy" to solve 5 X 3. The student was marked wrong for answering 5+5+5=15 because the answer was supposed to be 3+3+3+3+3 = 15.

Farmer Boy, author Laura Ingalls Wilder recounts how young Almanzo Wilder received an ox yoke for his ninth birthday so he could begin training ox calves by himself.

After hitching the calves to the yoke, his father left him alone to figure out how to train the young oxen to respond to simple commands. On his own, young Almanzo decided to use food as a reward, and had the calves obeying his commands in one session.

When I was a child, organized sports were not nearly as common as today. Groups of neighborhood kids would play pick-up sports, forming teams, picking captains and negotiating rules with no adult input at all. Before the last quarter of the twentieth century, it was common to send elementary school children, at what would now seem remarkably young ages, on errands to various businesses, often walking, biking, or taking public transportation by themselves.

When I was in first grade, my mother would send a permission slip to my school, allowing me to leave by myself, and walk on the sidewalk of a busy city street to the dentist for treatment. Children were expected to behave responsibly without constant adult supervision.

No More Independence. My, how times have changed!

Now parents arrange dates for play, and children are supervised constantly (and understandably, considering some of the ominous aspects of American society). Sports are adult-directed and children have no idea how to play without supervision. Children have few regular chores; parents are delighted if they just make their beds, and carry out an occasional bag of trash. Even homeschooling moms complain that students goof off as soon as mom's back is turned. This problem must be addressed early and consistently.

Much like our pioneer ancestors, the best way is to give our children real work—apart from their studies—show them how to do it, and then leave them to work on it alone. Work alongside of them at first, so they understand what needs to be done, and then leave them to it. Offer correction only when strictly necessary and praise them for a job well done. Follow a similar method for schoolwork.

If a child dawdles at math, for example, give him a reasonable amount of time to finish it, perhaps forty-five minutes. After that, the book is closed and put away. Give an adult consequence for neglecting one's work: the remainder of the assignment has to be finished during free time — TV, playtime, or even over the weekend. Don't argue and don't hover.

Children must learn to think and work by themselves

The value of independent work cannot be stressed too much. Constantly looking for direction from adults and approval from their peers is a recipe for producing gullible adults who will not take the initiative to look deeper into issues and decide for themselves what needs to be done. They will hesitate to make life decisions because they have made very few in the past.

The importance of encouraging young people to work independently is clear, and was evident until recent decades. Children who do not look to their peers for guidance and approval are far more likely to make prudent decisions. This may explain the comparably low levels of substance abuse and premature sexual activity among homeschooled adolescents, but benefits go beyond avoiding poor choices. Kids with a history of thinking for themselves learn that it is okay to fail. Experience has taught them to pick themselves up and look for solutions to the problem at hand. Seeking and finding answers to their own questions, with only occasional input from adults, builds self-confidence and focused initiative.

In the past, young people gained poise and satisfaction, not from constant, meaningless praise — Good job, Johnny! — but from the evident fact that their labor brought real value to the family farm or business. They could see, without being told, that milking the cows, feeding the pigs, and harvesting the crops put food on the table and cash in the pocket of the family farmer. Kids working in the family shop witnessed first-hand how much better the place looked because they had unloaded the truck and stocked the shelves with care. At a time when adult praise was often doled out at a miserly rate, kids needed it a whole lot less because they learned first-hand the significance of a job well done.

All of these benefits are becoming increasingly important in the United States at this time in history. Not that long ago, and still today in other cultures, extended families, close-knit communities, and local houses of worship gave needed aid to the elderly, the disabled or persons experiencing a crisis. That society is quickly disintegrating, leaving many Americans dependent on government.

You give your children a tremendous advantage by encouraging traits of independent thought, confidence, and self-reliance. There's a saying I picked up from my blue-collar forebears, "If you want a helping hand, you'll find one on the end of your arm."

Make sure your children know where to find their helping hands.

The Sixth Theme

Energetic Physical Sports Are not a Luxury

As a teenager, [George] Washington loved two things, dancing and horseback riding. ... Both studies paid off tremendously for the future president because the overpowering grace they communicated to his actions, a grace which counterpointed his large size, allowed him to physically command any gathering. Thanks to his twin obsessions, he bore his responsibilities with the aspect of a champion athlete, and that saved his life during the Revolution when a British sharpshooter drew a bead but found himself unable to pull the trigger because his target bore itself so magnificently.

John Taylor Gatto

John Taylor Gatto's sixth theme is that **students in prestigious private schools are encouraged to play "energetic" sports.** "Physical activity is not a way to blow off steam, but it is absolutely the only way to confer grace on the human presence, and that grace translates into power and money later on." Sports teach you practice in handling pain, and in dealing with emergencies

I've been touting the benefits students derive from lots of fresh air and exercise for years, but I have to admit that Gatto gave me a new insight.

Let me share seven of my own best reasons to get your kids moving and then I'll reveal the three reasons that Mr. Gatto gives. (Just to define some terms here, "energetic sports" include both playing on an organized team, like

Little League or AYSO soccer, as well as badminton or flag football on your side lawn. It might also include energetic arts, like marching band or dance.)

1. Build Focus and Attention

In 2009, researchers at the University of Illinois at Champaign-Urbana, looked at the effect moderate exercise has on 9 and 10-year-old boys and girls. They observed that after just 30 minutes of moderate exercise walking on a treadmill, the students performed better on both academic and cognitive testing. [4]

My own experience confirms this finding. When children run around, get their blood pumping, and fill their lungs with fresh air, they seem better able to concentrate and apply themselves to the task at hand when they turn to schoolwork. In former times, children got plenty of exercise walking a few miles to school and doing their chores; nevertheless, schools still insisted on recess. In our own times, kids spend hours staring at TV and computer screens, and often making their beds is the most vigorous activity of the day. Concerned parents need to provide physical activity in a more purposeful manner.

2. Practice Makes Perfect

Researchers have studied "masters," those who have reached the top of their fields in various areas of performance, including sports, the arts, and the game of chess. Interestingly, the "masters" consider innate ability and talent to be relatively unimportant when compared to

---

[4] https://news.illinois.edu/blog/view/6367/205988

abilities and skills acquired through hard work. They claim that thousands of hours of deliberate practice and training are necessary to reach the highest levels of performance. [5]

A figure skater may fall on the ice a hundred times before successfully landing an axel jump. Basketball players spend hours in front of a hoop practicing their shots. Budding fielders practice throwing and catching until they perfect getting the batter out. A desire to excel at a particular sport requires hard work, discipline and focus: qualities that also lend themselves to successful academics — and leadership.

3. Learn to Win and Lose Graciously and Keep it in Perspective

My son Chris's 13-year-old Pony League team came in first in the state competition. The following year, despite all their talent and hard work, they took second place. This was a big disappointment for the boys, but after the final game, they shook hands with the victors and congratulated them.

After the game, we all went out for ice cream. After all, there are real problems in the world: children dying of preventable diseases, Christians martyred for the faith, and whole countries living in famine. A lost baseball game is no big deal. Being able to see the big picture helps one develop a gracious attitude.

Good sportsmanship discourages being a sore loser, a particularly unattractive trait in sports, business, and life.

---

[5] http://projects.ict.usc.edu/itw/gel/EricssonDeliberatePracticePR93.pdf

4. Learn to Play by the Rules

No matter what, three strikes and the batter is out. No amount of whining gets him a fourth strike. A figure skater cannot scoot around the ice on her backside and call it a spin. No player can touch a soccer ball with hands except the goalie. Organized sports come with some pretty rigid regulations. Every member of the team plays by the same rules; even an uncoordinated first baseman has to catch the ball. Children learn that rules apply to all, and success follows those who follow rules.

Children playing pick-up sports in their backyards often create their own rules. Carefully considering the talent pool, available space and equipment resources, and weighing fairness, constitute a valuable exercise in management. Natural leadership is often developed in team sports.

5. Avoid the Devil's Workshop

Read *Farmer Boy* by Laura Ingalls Wilder to learn how hard a nine-year old had to work on the family farm in the mid-19th century. Little Almanzo had to wake before daylight to labor at his chores, walk over a mile in the icy upstate New York winter to school, walk home again as dusk descended, and then do his evening chores without even entering his home for a quick snack.

By contrast, school-age kids today have an awful lot of time on their hands. Too often they fill it by staring at a TV or computer screen watching useless nonsense. Idle hands are the devil's workshop and as they get older, bored kids often find trouble. Sports offer a wholesome and healthy alternative.

6. Win the Weight War

Currently about one in three U.S. children is overweight or obese. Extraordinarily, American doctors are now diagnosing school-age children with Type II diabetes, high blood pressure and elevated cholesterol, conditions previously considered a consequence of aging. Certainly, superior nutrition plays a role, but without doubt, playing at sports helps fight the fat. Shut the TV off, disconnect the video games and get those kids moving. High energy levels, a product of good health, are essential to success.

7. Play to the Crowd

It's the bottom of the ninth. The game is tied, two outs with bases loaded, as the batter approaches home plate. Both the pitcher and batter will give it their all, and the fielders will be ready to make a play. In just a few minutes, one team will be thrilled and the other dejected, and all of this takes place in front of a crowd. This situation, and thousands of others in team sports, teaches kids to give their best in front of an audience that may or may not be friendly. In a similar way, leaders in government and business need to be able to pitch their ideas to a crowd, all the while keeping their cool.

And now, here are three more reasons for students to engage in energetic sports from master teacher John Taylor Gatto:

8. Learn to Handle Pain

My girls played softball, and every so often one would get "stitched," hit by a pitched ball, hard enough to leave an imprint of the stitches from the ball on their skin.

Spectators and teammates would encourage them to "shake it off" because "there's no crying in softball." Everyone claps when an injured player gets up and walks off the field. Learning to calmly deal with pain, and continue towards a goal despite it, is a trait that is useful in every walk of life. John Taylor Gatto considers it essential in a leader.

9. Learn to Deal with Emergencies

The starting quarterback is injured, and the team has to get by with his replacement. The umpire calls a wide strike zone, and the batters have to adjust. Without warning, the music stops in the middle of the figure skater's long program. The unexpected crops up all the time in sports and players must simply deal with it. The ability to think on one's feet and adjust quickly to changing circumstances is crucial in a potential leader.

10. Learn to be a Calm & Confident Leader Who Inspires Confidence in Others

"Energetic physical sports are not a luxury, or a way to blow off steam, but they are absolutely the only way to confer grace on the human presence, and that grace translates into power and money later on."

Of course! Why didn't I think of that?

We have all seen this grace in soldiers whose physical presence has been honed by vigorous training and the Manual of Arms. True leaders dominate a room when they enter it — by their very presence. People pay attention to them. They attract the notice and loyalty of those around them by their calm, confident demeanor. They possess a control of their body and emotions that they learned through years of playing physical sports.

They are leaders.

The Seventh Theme

Develop a Complete Theory of Access to Any Workplace

...[j]ust 13 elite boarding schools educated 10 percent of all directors of large American business corporations and 15 percent of all the directors who held three or more directorships. These schools collectively graduated less than 1000 students a year. More spectacular pedagogy than that is hard to imagine.

John Taylor Gatto

In his younger days, my husband was a percussionist who played in a New York City band with Carmine Coppola, a musician and composer who won an Oscar and Golden Globe Award for his work on such films as *The Godfather* and *The Black Stallion*.

His son is renowned film director, Francis Ford Coppola, and his daughter is Talia Shire, perhaps best remembered as Adrian Balboa in the *Rocky* series of films.

Carmine's grandchildren Sofia Coppola and Nicolas Cage have both won numerous awards in the entertainment industry, as have two of his son-in-laws. A talented family, no doubt, but any reasonable person would presume that access to movers and shakers in the industry certainly offered members of the Coppola family opportunities denied to other entertainers who may be equally as talented.

Connections count!

But what about the rest of us: those of us with no friends and relatives in influential places?

Master teacher John Taylor Gatto addresses this issue in his fourteen themes of prestigious private schools: schools that design their curriculum around a central purpose of developing leaders for government, industry and the professions. Gatto believes that each student must develop a **"complete theory of access to any workplace"**.

In other words, those of us hailing from more humble backgrounds need to develop confidence and some strategies to help our children get to where they want to go. These simple steps may help.

Prepare them when they are young

Unlike the "free range" kids of my youth, children today have shockingly few unsupervised interactions with others. One essential aim of parenting is preparing our kids to meet the world outside our doors by themselves.

Starting with toddlers, have them interact frequently with extended family, friends, and neighbors. At first, you may have to provide them with words to use, "Before you leave, make sure you say thank you to Billy's mom for having you over."

A bit older, give them opportunities to tackle some of these occasions on their own. "Run over to Mrs. Smith's car and ask her if she needs help carrying her packages." Little by little, have them speak to strangers in a safe setting. "Ask the man at the counter if the prescription for Jones is ready." "Run inside and ask the lady at the front desk what time they close."

Teach your children how to use the telephone, look

up numbers in contacts, call, and speak to others using proper telephone etiquette. Start with friends and family. "Hi, Aunt Betsy, this is Matt. We're on our way, but Mom asked me to call and say we'll be about ten minutes late." Later, have them schedule their own medical and dental appointments, or to find out if a store carries a particular product.

Step one is ensuring that our children can interact with confidence and grace outside their immediate circle.

Teach them self-reliance

During school years, let your children know that they are responsible for their own plans. If Billy wants to join a soccer league, ask him how he plans to pay for it and get there. (Hint: The answer is NOT Dad will pay and Mom will drive.)

One answer might be, "I can earn half of the $70 fee babysitting (mowing lawns, raking leaves, etc.), Mom. What can I do around the house to earn the rest? Sammy on the next block is joining the team too, and we plan to ride our bikes together."

Figuring out how to get to where they want to go through their own efforts gives children confidence.

Letting go can be a bit nerve-racking for Mom and Dad, but is absolutely essential. By their early teens, my children had learned to safely navigate Chicago's "L," the city's commuter train line, to go downtown for lunch, shopping, or a Cubs game.

Most of them had flown, by themselves, to other cities to visit family and friends. One daughter flew alone to Santiago, Chile when she was fifteen, and spent a month with her friend's family. All of my children had jobs and were responsible for their own clothing, travel, and entertainment expenses.

They learned to rely on themselves and to understand that they can reach their goals through their own efforts.

Encourage them to get involved in their communities

No later than high school make sure that your children learn to actively pursue their dreams and not wait for opportunity to come knocking at the door.

Perhaps your little Johnny is interested in politics. Encourage him to volunteer during campaign time. Let him learn firsthand about campaign calls, placing signs, and getting voters out. Let him meet local politicians. Perhaps he will be totally enchanted, or turned off; but either way, he will gain an understanding of how the process works.

Maybe your Janie has trouble finding suitable literature at your local public library. Find out when the Library Board meets and urge her to attend. She will gain an understanding of how such meetings are run by rules of order, and how small groups of people often control crucial aspects of daily life in a community.

If Joey is interested in becoming a plumber or carpenter, have him call around to local companies and ask how to get started. Many professionals are happy to speak to young people and sometimes even offer them a job as helpers on jobsites.

If recent history in Catholic homeschooling is an indicator, some of your children may be considering a vocation to the priesthood or religious life. Various religious orders and dioceses have programs — often free or at a very reasonable rate — to help a person learn more about a life of service to the Church.

The rector of the minor seminary here in Chicago offers free classes in theology to anyone interested. Many religious orders host "come and see" days or retreats to inform potential applicants and introduce them to their order's rule. Have your child call, write, or email vocation directors to learn more.

The Whole World is a Classroom

It's no coincidence that our sixth president, John Quincy Adams was the son of our second, Founding Father John Adams. Our nation's twenty-third president, Benjamin Harrison was the grandson of the ninth, William Henry Harrison and the great-grandson of Benjamin Harrison V, a signer of the *Declaration of Independence.* Closer to our own time, former Florida Governor Jeb Bush could potentially win the trifecta for his family, as both his father and brother have already occupied the Oval Office.

Catholic homeschooling helps you provide your students a world-class education in your home, but God has provided them an even larger classroom. Encourage your children to follow their interests outside the home and learn more about the opportunities that are available.

Your community, your state, our country and the Catholic Church all need well-formed homeschool graduates to make a real difference.

The Eighth Theme

Proven Ways to Teach Your Kids Responsibility

Work in classrooms isn't significant work; it fails to satisfy real needs pressing on the individual; it doesn't answer real questions experience raises in the young mind; it doesn't contribute to solving any problem encountered in actual life. The net effect of making all schoolwork external to individual longings, experiences, questions, and problems is to render the victim listless.

John Taylor Gatto

More than ever, American society needs leaders who are well formed, not only academically, but also spiritually. Faithful Catholics will also see a need for energetic young people to enter the priesthood and consecrated life, and to serve our parishes and dioceses as faithful laymen. Gatto's eighth theme considers, **"Responsibility as an utterly essential part of the curriculum."**

John Taylor Gatto notes that children from wealthy, influential families are taught, "always to grab responsibility when it is offered and always to deliver more than is asked for." In the case of prep school kids, responsibility might include caring for a horse. That is probably out of our reach, but here are some ways to develop a strong sense of responsibility and purpose in your children.

Chores, chores, and more chores

From their earliest years, teach your children to care, first for their own needs, and then for the necessities of the household. Even toddlers can put their soiled clothing in a hamper, stow their pajamas under their pillows and their toys in the toy box. They can carry their dinner dishes to the sink, and help load and unload the dishwasher.

As they enter their school years, teach your children to perform every task that needs to be done in your home and yard. Children should be able to scramble eggs for themselves and their siblings, put together a salad, and bake brownies. They should know how to clean safely and properly every room in the house, including bathrooms, and have the regular responsibility to keep some of these rooms shipshape.

Outside, teach them to water the garden, weed, and when they are old enough to understand safety precautions, mow and edge the lawn. One child should have the weekly job of cleaning out and vacuuming the family car.

Do not tolerate any whining! Accepting household responsibilities builds a hard work ethic and confidence in children.

Seek opportunities to work and serve in the community

Your children should develop reputations as the "go to" kids in the neighborhood when someone needs a job done right. Encourage them to have small businesses babysitting, walking dogs for working neighbors, raking leaves, shoveling walks, and bringing in mail for people on vacation.

They will learn to interact with others and see that their best efforts are rewarded.

Encourage your kids to regard service to others as a way of life. Let them "grab responsibility" by carrying in bags for neighbors when they see them pull up with a car full of groceries and kids.

Have them ask elderly neighbors if they need food or medicine picked up, or some yard work done. Are there any public institutions, like the library or community hospital, that need volunteers? A simple search will often reveal numerous ways to serve their own friends and neighbors.

Help out at Church

Does your parish have missalettes, those periodicals we use to follow along at Mass? Have your younger children take just a few minutes after Mass, go through the pews, return the missalettes to the spot they belong, at the end of the pews or in racks.

As they get older, encourage them to become altar servers, readers, religious education assistants, members of the choir or altar society, and ushers. Is there a pro-life group your teen can join? Look for ways to take on even more responsibilities. Perhaps your child can help schedule the altar servers and email the list. Parish groups are always looking for helpers to set up refreshments and pitch in with clean up.

High school students will find many opportunities to serve the church. Parishes often send a bus to Washington D.C. every year for the March for Life. Perhaps your teen can man a table after Mass signing up marchers and collecting donations to defray costs.

In Chicago, an organized group of Catholic teens crash pro-abortion rallies. What a refreshingly wholesome contrast they are to the vulgar, offensive speakers and marchers from the other side. When my daughter was in high school, she joined the Appalachian Service Project, rehabbing houses in poor rural areas. In one local parish, teens deliver meals to the sick or elderly. One of my daughters volunteers with the Little Sisters of the Poor. No matter where you live, there are always opportunities to serve in the Church.

Seek Leadership Roles

Often clubs, scouts, and other organizations are looking for leaders because members hesitate to take on additional duties. Urge your children to fill the leadership void. Help them learn the skills they will need as part of their home schooling. Maybe they need to keep track of club expenses on an Excel spreadsheet, or send out group emails.

Pass on any knowledge you may have. If you never learned to use these tools yourself, you can always find free tutorials online. Members of organizations will need interpersonal skills to build support and consensus within their organizations. Members will have to learn time management. Someone must be in charge, must captain the ship. It may as well be your child.

Leadership looks great on a college application and an employment resume. It is also terrific training for future education, jobs, and family management.

Requiring your children to take on more responsibility comes with the added bonus of giving busy homeschooling moms and dads some much needed practical help.

Everyone wins!

The Ninth Theme

Arrive at a Personal Code of Standards

It's difficult to imagine anyone who lacks an understanding of Western spirituality regarding themselves as educated. And yet, American schools have been forbidden to enter this arena even in a token way since 1947.

John Taylor Gatto

In his ninth theme, John Taylor Gatto says each young person must arrive **at a personal code of standards** and that developing this code is a "long range, comprehensive thing that needs to be checked regularly." Students must be encouraged to formulate and adopt a personal code of standards in production, behavior and morality.

Understanding a Personal Code in a Catholic Sense

This theme may seem to be a bit suspect to some Catholic parents. After all, why develop a *personal* code of standards? Shouldn't our children live according to *Catholic* standards?

Studying the doctrines and history of the Church closely, especially the saints, answers that question. We realize the Church has always been characterized by a proper understanding of diversity and that diversity applies here. We must all, for example, maintain a detachment from material things. That's clear from both the Seventh and Tenth Commandments, as well as Our Lord's exhortation to "Consider the lilies of the field." Not all of us, however, are called to live without a clothes closet or hot water, as Mother Teresa's Missionaries of Charity do. Catholics must all care for the elderly, but not necessarily invite them into our homes as the Little Sisters of the Poor do.

Personal standards must always *start* with Catholic values, but those values will be *lived* differently in each individual.

In my application of Gatto's ninth theme to Catholic families, our children must first learn and integrate principles of Catholic daily life, but then develop — from them — a personal code of standards for living.

This could mean a commitment to the poor and elderly, devoting one's life to pro-life action, or dedicating oneself to furthering Catholic education. Perhaps as adults, our children will seek to better society through government service, or help keep our nation secure by joining the military. Perhaps they will bring beauty to our world as artists, musicians, dancers, or composers. But whatever pursuits our children aspire to, they must set high goals, develop plans to meet those goals, and then follow through enthusiastically. As they are working in their chosen fields, our children must be models of decency, hard work and fair play. They should be reliable, always meeting or exceeding their obligations, and their word should be their bond.

Gatto believes our children need high standards for three specific activities: production, behavior, and morality.

Standards of Production

What, you may well ask, are *children* expected to produce? A perfect score on a spelling test would be a good start. How about a well-thought-out book report with no grammatical errors?

When speaking of "production," and children, the "product" they are primarily responsible for is their schoolwork. The part we parents play is to insist that they do their best, always looking to improve.

Give your children a schedule of assignments every day, and insist that they will be done correctly and completely. Make sure that your students respect their efforts by presenting work that is neat with no obvious erasures or cross outs. Letters have to be on the line and numbers in careful columns. Make them redo sloppy or poorly executed assignments, but rave about their excellent work to Dad (in their hearing), and post it on the fridge.

A commitment to excellence in schoolwork will spill over into their household chores, the enthusiasm they bring to sports practice, musical performance, and their early attempts to earn some cash.

Behavior

Without doubt, it is the parents' job to ensure that their children know and obey the Ten Commandments and live according to Catholic values. On this we cannot waver.

The true task, however, is to inculcate these values and behaviors so that our children take ownership of their own actions. I think this is the "long range comprehensive thing that must be checked regularly" to which Gatto refers. It will take some time.

Parents spend their children's early years teaching the rules and insisting that they be obeyed. Around the age of reason, maybe seven-years-old, we need to start encouraging the children to police their own actions. They are absolutely capable of it. I started this process with questions.

What time do *you* think *you* should come home? Do you think this is your *best* work? Do *you* think that was a kind remark you made? I urged them to develop empathy for others. "How would *you* feel if someone said something like that to you?' I nudged them to the right answer, and Mom and Dad always had veto power, but questioning themselves about their own motives, actions, and words is one way to make children understand and take personal responsiblity for their behavior.

As the teen years approach, parents must seek to strike a balance between allowing our children independence while keeping them on the straight and narrow. I am convinced we cannot find this balance if we insist on a strictly enforced, rigid set of rules. We have to allow them to make their own plans, and some mistakes along the way, as long as they do not violate God's laws.

We give them lots of freedom and trust, and then we see them take an unwise turn. Time to pull in the reins. When my children would accuse me of not trusting them to make a decision about this or that (Piercing your belly button! Have you lost your mind?), I would remind them that I trust their good intentions, but their young judgment may be seriously lacking.

Nevertheless, the goal is not to inflict our sound judgment or good morals on our kids. The ultimate goal is for them to use their own sound judgment and strong values to police themselves.

Morality

Catholic homeschoolers have a unique opportunity to form our children's personal morality, and to lead them to adapt Catholic values as uniquely their own. The whole moral life can be summed up in four words: Do good; avoid evil. Parents spend the first part of their children's lives teaching them the difference through word, example, and religious studies.

As time goes on, we want them to understand not just what good is, but that they need to do good, and finally that they want to do good, all the time, even when no one else is looking.

Traditional Catholic practices will be a huge help with this endeavor. Teach your children to examine their consciences every night at bedtime. Here's an easy exam for the youngest children:

> Think of God, His name and day,
> Parents too, who care for you.
> Are you kind in every way?
> Pure and honest, truthful too?

Perhaps nothing will help your children grow in the moral life more than frequent Confession. Monthly is a minimum. Encourage their confessors to give them ongoing spiritual direction. Finally, a solid — single gender — retreat can be very beneficial, helping teens to refine their moral principles away from their everyday lives.

Encourage your children to develop strong values to live by. The Church, our nation and the world will reap the benefits.

The Tenth Theme

Ways Your Child Can Become Familiar with the Fine Arts

Gothic Architecture itself was invented out of sheer aspiration – the Gothic cathedral stands out like a lighthouse illuminating what is possible in the way of uncoerced human union. It provides a benchmark against which our own lives can be measured. At Rheims, the serfs and farmers and peasants filled gigantic spaces with the most incredible stained-glass windows in the world, but they never bothered to sign even one of them... After all these centuries they still announce what being human really means.

John Taylor Gatto

Cultural Capital

Gatto's tenth theme is that young people must have a comfortable familiarity with the fine arts, what he refers to as "cultural capital." **They must be familiar with the "master creations" of great artists in fields like "music, painting, dance, sculpture, design, architecture, literature and drama."**

His reasoning? "Apart from religion, the arts are the only way to transcend the animal materiality of our lives."

In the not too distant past, it was tough for families living apart from major cities to find opportunities to expose their children to the fine arts.

My children have enjoyed a great, if informal, music education at home from their dad, a former musician.

He must have done a great job as two daughters pursued musical studies after high school. Although raising twelve kids was not a recipe for disposable income, what little we did have often went for theatre tickets, and trips to other Fine Arts destinations.

Having lived all our lives around New York City and Chicago, my family has had the advantage of world class cultural institutions like Chicago's Lyric Opera, New York's Metropolitan Museum of Art, and of course theatre — on and off Broadway. The gap between cultural haves and have-nots has changed, however, thanks to videos and the Internet.

While I urge you to find opportunities for your children to experience live productions and personally see and hear great works, you can still offer them some rich cultural experiences right in your own home.

A word of caution: always exercise prudence when accessing anything on the Internet or on TV.

PBS

You can expose your children to great music, musical theatre, drama, dance and opera if you have a TV and computer.

An extensive number of world-class performances can be watched, and videos ordered if you search for "PBS Great Performances". *Great Performances* has been running on public broadcasting for over 40 years. The show has something for everyone.

YouTube

I just searched "YouTube Chicago Symphony Orchestra." There, you can listen to a changing list of complete world-class performances, excerpts from other great works, and discussion from top tier musicians.

And it's free!

On YouTube, I searched for "Broadway" and came across a five episode PBS series about American Broadway theatre. You can see and hear snippets of great performances with history and background.

You can search for Lang Lang, Yo Yo Ma, or Wynton Marsalis, and original cast performances of shows such as *Les Miserables* or *Newsies*. A simple search for "ballet" not only brought up performances, but explanations of basic ballet positions.

You can see top performances of all genres with just an Internet connection, always remembering to monitor your children when they are online.

Museum websites

I checked out four: The Louvre in Paris, London's National Gallery, The Metropolitan Museum of Art in New York City and the Art Institute of Chicago. The websites allow you look at some of the great works featured in these institutions. Better than that, they give some background and explanation for those of us who were not art history majors.

Websites have pictures and descriptions of some of the works, and short biographies of the artists. You might try the National Gallery in Washington, D. C., the Uffizi in

Florence, or the Prado in Madrid. In fact, your children might age out of homeschooling before you could visit a comprehensive list of art museum websites.

London's National Gallery has a "Picture of the Month" feature. When I visited, the painting was Titian's *Noli Me Tangere*. Your browser can translate the text on the Louvre website. The audio in the children's section seemed quite excellent, but unfortunately there is no English translation available.

The art museums offered, what seemed to me, the least satisfactory websites for learn-at-home purposes. A trip to the public library might be a better option for the visual arts.

Live Performances

Even if you live in suburban or rural areas, there are always opportunities to see some live performances. Most public and private high schools and community colleges have drama programs and put on plays. Some are quite professional. Many communities have local theatre companies. Private dance academies often have recitals for their students, and some of these can be excellent. If you are not sure if the show would be appropriate for children, you can almost always get information online or by calling the company.

Often localities host band concerts during the summer or on patriotic holidays. You can learn more about patriotic music by reading biographies of John Philip Sousa or George M. Cohan.

I found a six-minute video about John Phillip Sousa, by doing a simple Internet search, and also found a biography of George M Cohan that was considerably more accurate than the Jimmy Cagney movie *Yankee Doodle Dandy*.

Not sure what the difference is between a philharmonic orchestra and a concert band, or what the major sections of an orchestra are? You can look it all up online.

Architecture

The village I live in claims to have the highest number of architecturally significant buildings, per capita, in the United States. My kids certainly know the difference between Victorian and Prairie School, and they know more about Frank Lloyd Wright than the average American. If you live in a 20th century subdivision with less thrilling home styles, all is not lost.

An Internet search can bring you to a website that explains the differences in various styles of American homes. You can even learn the various subsets of styles, such as Queen Anne, Italianate, and stick style — all Victorians. There are many websites that offer online tours of many of our country's finest homes

Many of you live within driving distance of Catholic churches that are rich architectural resources. Usually, the older the church the lovelier it is, and often you can learn the history on the church website.

Resources are everywhere

As you can see, fine arts resources are almost limitless for anyone with a computer or public library. Let me add that when it comes to sacred art, Seton Home Study School gives students an education that compares—I would guess excels—that of any high-priced prep school.

Have your children look at the lists of artworks and artists in the back of many books and research them at the library. Notice that the back covers of Seton books feature examples of the finest church architecture and many of these churches are in cities where you live or visit.

Turn off mindless television shows and hip-hop music. Expose your students to the best entertainment. Let them understand that sacred music is more than just the hymns they hear at church on Sunday. Let them hear Handel's *Messiah*.

Do not miss any opportunity to give your children knowledge and love of the fine arts. It will enrich their lives.

The Eleventh Theme

Stimulate the Power of Accurate Observation and Recording

[An elite public school classroom] still falls far short of the goals of elite private boarding schools, almost as if the very best government schools are willing to offer is only a weak approximation of the leadership style of St. Paul's or Groton.[6] What fascinates me most is the cold-blooded quality of this shortfall because Groton's expectations cost almost nothing to meet on a different playing field – say a home school setting.... Virtually everyone could be educated the Groton way for less money than the average public school costs.

John Taylor Gatto

Among the British Upper classes, Gatto asserts, it was axiomatic that if persons could not accurately draw what they had seen, then they could not have actually viewed it properly. Drawing was seen not as an upper-class pastime, but rather as a method to sharpen perception.

John Taylor Gatto's eleventh principle of prestigious private schools is **to develop students' ability to accurately observe what is around them, and to record their observations with precision.** Children may "record"

---

[6] Groton and St. Paul's are two East Coast private prep schools. Groton in Massachusetts charged $56,700 for tuition fees, room and board for the 2014-15 school year. St. Paul's in New Hampshire charged $52,200.

the results of their inspections in several ways, including recounting them orally, writing about them, or drawing them.

Observation and Recording during Preschool Years

Parents naturally work on this skill with preschool children, by asking them the name of body parts or animals at the zoo, to use two examples. Expand vocabulary,[7] improve observation and teach oral recounting by asking your toddler to describe his arm, for example, in greater detail: hand, finger (thumb and pinky), fingernails, knuckles, wrist, forearm, elbow and shoulder.

Ask him if his hand is bigger than Daddy's or smaller than baby sister's. A typical two or three-year old can certainly recognize a car. Now ask her to locate the windshield, steering wheel, glove compartment, tire, hood, engine, and trunk. Ask her what color the car is and if there are any other cars like it on your street.

Try to build detailed observation by teaching description and variety. If your child points to a pretty flower, identify it as a tulip or a pansy. Ask the child to describe it. It's a pink tulip, or a pretty tulip, or a drooping tulip.

Get a picture book from the library of local birds and look for them in your neighborhood. Again have a conversation with your children. Male cardinals are red while females are a plainer maroon; it is building a nest; it is singing; it is lively. Use lots of prepositions. The robin is on the branch, or under it, or next to it.

---

[7] Research indicates that limited word knowledge is a major handicap for children from disadvantaged homes, leading to the obvious conclusion that a wide vocabulary offers a distinct advantage.

Keep colored pencils, crayons and paper on hand, and when the nature walk is over, ask your children to draw the flower or the bird that you talked about. Press them to add more details. For example, "The cardinal was sitting on a branch, why don't you draw that."

School Years

Students learn simple paragraph writing in the second grade, so this is a good time to add descriptive paragraphs. Ask your child to look closely at your china cabinet, for example, and then draw a picture of it. Using techniques from English class, help the student write a short paragraph. Insist on close observations and a detailed description.

A 2nd grader should be able to note that the china in the cabinet is blue with a pattern of white flowers. They might describe wine glasses with a flower design cut into the glass, and write that there are three shelves in the cabinet. Can they draw and color a dinner plate with that pattern?

By 4th grade, your student should be able to both observe more closely and record more details. Now they might describe the cabinet as made of dark wood with two glass panels on the door and three drawers beneath the glass. They can identify the blue china as Wedgwood, with a raised white flowered pattern on dishes with scalloped edges. Wine glasses are made of etched crystal with an ivy design. Perhaps that child could attempt an accurate drawing of the cabinet.

Gatto stresses the desirability of drawing to observe and record, but many of us have little natural artistic ability and no idea how to teach this skill. All is not lost. A simple Internet search revealed a large number of online drawing resources, some free, many others quite reasonably priced.

Seton Books sells a collection of videos by Ginger Himes to help with this. If you are interested in adding drawing to your school day, not just as part of art class, but also to teach careful observation and recording, check out Ms. Himes's offerings.

Speaking of Seton and Art

The beautiful reproductions of master paintings and stained glass windows in the Seton workbooks delight the eye while teaching students an appreciation for the best of Christian art as well as important religious lessons. Photographs of historic churches teach students to value Catholic architecture. An added educational advantage of these illustrations is the opportunity to look closely and study the details of each one.

For example, there is a lovely oil painting of the *Education of the Virgin* on page one of the third grade spelling book. The Blessed Mother is a child, kneeling on a red cushion next to her elderly mother who is holding a scroll with Hebrew characters. St Joachim is looking over their shoulders and angels are watching from heaven.

Other women in the picture are working on what appears to be textiles, and fabric has spilled from a basket to the floor. One woman seems to be warming her hands over an unseen fire. What do we see that causes us to think that? The architecture looks more like a grand public building than a private home.

Focusing on visual details of paintings will help children develop observation and thinking skills. Interestingly, this can translate into higher skill levels in seemingly unrelated subjects like spelling and reading comprehension because children develop better visual recall.

Benefits Beyond Education

It is easy to understand how the ability to carefully observe and reproduce or recount observations is important to developing, not only excellent students, but also first-rate citizens and future leaders.

A successful professional, business owner, priest or religious, each requires the ability to carefully assess a situation by closely scrutinizing it. Then the lawyer has to be able to articulate the legal question, the priest the theological issue, the entrepreneur the business need.

People who have this aptitude will go far in life. It will come more naturally to some than others; nevertheless, it can be taught to everyone.

Prestigious private schools teach it and so can homeschooling parents.

The Twelfth Theme

The Ability to Deal with Challenges of All Sorts

What drove the nineteenth century school world ... was a society rich with concepts like duty, hard work, responsibility, and self-reliance...

John Taylor Gatto

John Taylor Gatto's twelfth theme, and his personal favorite, is **to instill in children the ability to deal courageously with challenges of all sorts.** Life can be tough and unfair, but history is full of leaders who dealt with problems head on, often using them as a springboard to future success.

Tailor the Challenges to the Child

Homeschoolers often modify educational materials to meet their children's unique learning needs. Teaching our children to meet and overcome personal obstacles with courage and determination is also a customized process. Is your daughter painfully shy? Push her into social situations on a regular basis. Give her words she needs to greet and converse with others. Have her give oral presentations as part of her schoolwork.

Does your son have trouble sitting still and paying attention? Don't treat this as an incurable condition; rather consider ways your son can overcome this problem. Give him activities, such as Lincoln Logs™, legos™, and puzzles that build concentration. Let him start with short bursts of schoolwork, but add ten minutes every couple of weeks until he can apply himself for longer periods.

Are your children uncoordinated? Have them practice throwing and catching, or dribbling a basketball. Are they lazy? Shut off the TV and give them extra chores. Are they frightened of needles? Bring them to the doctor every time someone gets a vaccination or blood test, so they see needles are nothing more than a tiny sting.

Years ago, when my three-year old daughter was terrified of dogs, my husband brought one home from a shelter. She overcame her fear in a matter of days. Practice and familiarity will help your children gain confidence in overcoming their fears and struggles.

Teach Courage

Until fairly recent times, physical pain was a common occurrence during childhood. Before vaccinations, children caught a host of childhood diseases, many of them quite painful. In spring and fall, farm kids worked planting and harvesting until their muscles ached. Students walked miles to school, in all weather. Many had jobs both before and after school to supplement family income. In the days before electricity, running water, and central heat, children performed back-breaking labor hauling wood and water. Tired and achy, these children for the most part stood up, dusted themselves off, and realized that the pain was not that big a deal. By adulthood, they had learned to take lots of discomfort in their stride.

In our own time, novice ice skaters may throw themselves into the air and smash on the hard, cold ice dozens, maybe hundreds, of times before they land their first axel jump. They stand up and try again. Water skiers fall in the lake and swallow water all the time. They spit it out, and get back on their skis. Batters get whacked with a pitched ball; they shake off the pain and take their base. All of these exemplify the correct attitude to foster grit and determination.

Children need to learn to take discomfort, even real pain, in their stride. It is a fact of life, and no one can hope to escape it. When children learn to handle discomfort, they build the virtue of fortitude or courage. When the courageous are knocked flat by an obstacle or illness, they stand right back up, shake it off, and get back in the race.

Why Must *Students* be Courageous?

My personal experience on social media makes me share John Taylor Gatto's admiration for inculcating courage as a key to academic success. We have all seen it. A mom posts that her seven-year-old son dawdles over schoolwork, gives her a hard time, and even throws tantrums. Other moms will advise her that seven is way too young for school work, Mom should drop the idea of schoolwork altogether, and let him have fun all day.

Maybe he needs a totally new curriculum, attuned to his special needs. Others will recommend that he be tested for ADHD. More than one will suggest eliminating gluten, or food coloring, or sugar from his diet, or giving him an herbal supplement, or a vitamin supplement, or treating his condition with essential oils. The list goes on and on.

I'm a big believer in the necessity of nutritious diets coupled with plenty of fresh air and exercise as important to academic success, and some small percentage of children do have a diagnosable learning disorder. That said, Mom might first want to look at the obvious issue: little boys have lots of energy and would rather play then work. Sonny is hoping Mom will let him out if he throws a fit.

Learning the 4 R's (reading, 'riting, 'rithmetic, and religion) is really important, so Sonny has to learn how to sit still and apply himself for reasonable periods of time. No complaining allowed, and certainly no tantrums! Let him work for smaller intervals and build his concentration skills over time. Little boys are super practical, so let him see that much of what he is learning will lead to fun and adventures outside of school. He will know by how many points his soccer team won the game, or be able to read for himself how Ethan Allen and the Green Mountain Boys took Fort Ticonderoga in the "name of the Great Jehovah and the Continental Congress."

Does your daughter struggle in math? Your Facebook buddies can recommend dozens of math programs they claim are better, more effective, more engaging, and more fun than the one you use. But if she were struggling with learning the piano, her teacher would recommend more practice, not a different placement of the keys. The solution, very likely, is to apply herself with more diligence to a subject she does not enjoy. She will not necessarily be happy about it, but that's the point.

Sometimes all of us have to do something we find boring or distasteful, or downright painful to achieve an important goal. (Think of giving birth!) When the goal is a worthy one — and academic excellence is essential — those who shoulder on will meet success.

Look to the Saints

When thinking about instilling courage in our children, we Catholics can receive inspiration from the saints, especially the martyrs. Long before St. Thomas More climbed the scaffold in the Tower of London, he was in the habit of denying himself pleasure and actively practicing penance. After a lifetime of achievement, when the time came to stand up for the truth, Thomas had the courage to die for it.

If Tudor England seems a bit remote, let's never forget that Christians are being martyred right now in the Middle East by terrorists from the Islamic State. No one is dying in the United States but citizens are being punished for following Christian principles.

Just consider that the states of Illinois and Massachusetts shut down Catholic Charities adoption and foster care agencies because they would not place children with same gender couples. In several states, Christian bakeries, florists and catering houses are being sued, in some cases for both business and personal assets, because they refuse to provide services to so-called gay weddings. The United States Air Force censored a chaplain for writing an article that included the adage, often attributed to President Dwight Eisenhower, "There are no atheists in foxholes."

New York's Mount Sinai Hospital coerced a Catholic nurse to participate in a late term abortion or lose her job and even her license to practice.

Have we given our children the courage they will need to stand up for the truth no matter how terrible the consequence? When we teach our children to say no to themselves, and to accept whatever life throws at them with fortitude and determination, we prepare them for leadership in the classroom and in life.

The Thirteenth Theme

Develop a Habit of Caution in Reasoning to Conclusion

Individuality, family and community, on the other hand, are, by definition, expressions of singular organization, never of "one-right-way thinking on a grand scale. Private time is absolutely essential if a private identity is going to develop, and private time is equally essential to the development of a code of private values, without which we aren't really individuals at all. ... Without these freedom has no meaning.

John Taylor Gatto

John Taylor Gatto's thirteenth theme — **encourage children to develop a habit of caution in reasoning to conclusion** — is especially important in our own times. Many Americans base their opinions, and their votes, on short articles they read on the Internet, interviews they see on television, or even views of their "friends" on social media.

Low Information Students

In politics, this situation has produced the "low information voter," and the issue of caution, or its lack, in forming conclusions is certainly one where private prep schools, and hopefully our homeschools, will distinguish themselves from America's public schools.

My own experience with government schools confirms this situation. For ten years, I was a pro-life educator in New York State.

Public schools would contact me — often so-called "talented and gifted" classes — and ask me to address the students presenting arguments against abortion or euthanasia. Educators would also ask a representative of a group like Planned Parenthood or The Hemlock Society to come in and give opposite points of view. Then, typically, the "talented and gifted" students were asked to write a persuasive essay supporting whichever argument seemed stronger.

Think of it. Based on a couple of forty-minute classes, these students were asked — no, they were required — to form and express opinions about life and death issues, and then presumably were graded on their answers. These types of assignments are common in public school, and many of them have a strong political agenda dictated by forces outside students' families and religious systems. Students are asked to write papers on global warming for example, advocate for more lavishly funded government social welfare programs, or even decide who gets tossed off the lifeboat so others can live.

While principles of Catholic dogma are never up for debate, many questions are more prudential than dogmatic. We should teach our students to form opinions cautiously and humbly enough to change their minds when circumstances warrant it. Our children need to gain the virtue of humility and be willing to admit that what they thought to be true needs to be looked at again.

Even better, they might reserve judgment entirely until they have more facts or until a decision must be made. It's okay to say, "I am not sure what I believe about capital punishment, hydraulic fracturing, or educational vouchers. I need to know more about the subject before I form an opinion, and my opinion might change as new information comes to light." How can we help our children develop the humility to reserve judgment, as well as the intellectual curiosity to search for the truth? Here are some ideas to get you started.

Turn off the screens

Very little on TV, on social media or in a video game will inform your child about the world around them. Children are passive recipients of what passes for entertainment, and virtually no in-depth thought is required of them. Screen time is a huge vacuum sucking precious, unrepeatable opportunities to ponder and learn right out of your kid's brains.

Unless they are watching nature shows, a dramatic or musical performance, or practicing their math facts, they are probably wasting their time. Shut off the screens and get out some quality books. Better yet, throw them outdoors where they can observe real life situations.

Non-fiction will open your children's eyes to the world around them.

Benjamin Franklin said, "An investment in knowledge pays the best interest." Learning about the world by studying history, art, music, or science engages the child's mind and perks curiosity. Children discover that really smart people make mistakes, and knowledge can change over time.

Reading biographies of famous military, political, or scientific figures is both informational and inspirational. Those destined for greatness often walked a path that was not at all straight, requiring them to reevaluate their ideas and their plans. Students come to understand that like prominent figures, they must, from time to time, upgrade their understanding, make better decisions, or understand that they can reserve judgment.

Grammar aids in more than writing!

At some point, many public schools sharply limited the amount of time students spend studying traditional grammar, claiming that it did not aid in composition skills. As often happens, government schools make expansive claims with little evidence, and there has been no massive improvement in student writing.[8] Studying intensive grammar, however, accomplishes more than making a student's compositions easier to read. Young people learn to think logically and precisely when working on grammar assignments. Grammar does not lend itself to fuzzy thinking.

Is that noun common or proper; singular or plural; masculine, feminine or neuter; subjective, objective or possessive? Where does it belong in the sentence diagram? Is it used as the subject, predicate nominative, appositive, direct object, or object of the preposition? Is that phrase used as an adverb or adjective?

---

[8] Sadly this situation may even worsen. Some educators are claiming that, with the wide acceptance of word processing programs and smart phones, students now need neither grammar nor spelling skills.

Too many public and Catholic schools have abandoned intensive grammar, and it shows in more than sloppy writing. Thinking has become pretty sloppy too.

Analyzing literature

High school students frequently complain about literary analysis assignments in their English classes, but this work is key to what is often described as "critical thinking." Reading increasingly complex literature and analyzing elements of plot, theme, conflict, characterization, and setting force students to think about their reading. In addition to building writing skills, essay writing requires students to organize their thoughts in a logical manner, formulate one or more central ideas, back up their assertions with facts from the story, and draw conclusions. Vague thinking will simply not cut it.

To Sum Up

Turning off electronics, learning about the world around them, reading biographies of great men and women of history, studying high quality literature, and even diagramming sentences work to impress on children the humility to realize that their own talents and abilities still need to develop.

Analyzing what they learn, filtering it through Catholic values, and employing logical thinking patterns help children realize that they may need more information than they have. These help to develop habits of caution when reasoning.

Allow me to make one final suggestion: put your children's minds to the test — put them on the spot. If they complain that the kid next door is not fun to play with, ask them to give their reasons, then press them to say something nice about him.

If your children want to accompany their friends to the movies, ask them to find out how it is rated, and give you three reasons why they should be allowed to go. Ask them if they can think of any reasons they should not be allowed to go.

If they tell you video games are a good use of their time, ask them how they know that and ask them to prove it. Ask them to list reasons why video games may be bad for them. Teach them to look at both sides of an issue to understand that both sides may have valid points.

A bit of thought and you will see that even the youngest children can be helped to reason carefully. Guide your children to be the high-information voters, and leaders, of tomorrow.

The Fourteenth Theme

How to Develop (& Test) Judgment in Children

All the pathologies [of mass government schooling] we've considered come about in large measure because the lessons of school prevent children from keeping important appointments with themselves and with their families to learn lessons in self-motivation, perseverance, self-reliance, courage, dignity, and love – and lessons in service to others, too, which are among the key lessons of home and community life.

John Taylor Gatto

John Taylor Gatto's final theme is to **encourage constant development and testing of judgments.** Allow students to consider an issue and perhaps come to a tentative conclusion. Then, they must form a habit of keeping an eye on that prediction, continuing to research in order to refine and enrich available information. Finally, they must be ready to change their minds and revamp their point of view if subsequent facts or events warrant it.

This theme is certainly connected to Catholic values. A good Catholic must always search for all that is true, even when the truth given is not evident. Our Faith requires us to refine our facts and conclusions through diligent research and the filter of Church teaching. We must acquire the virtue of humility, being willing to admit we might have been wrong and to change our point of view.

These good habits can be learned early in life and reinforced as years go by.

Start Early

Often, the first judgments our children make concern their playmates. "He's mean." "She never shares her toys." They may draw positive conclusions. "Those new kids, who just moved in, are so much fun."

Often their impressions may be true at the time, but may not be proof of lasting character traits. Parents need to help young children realize that first impressions must be tested again and again.

The "fun" kid on the block may be rude or have fun at the expense of others. Even little children have a strong sense of justice. You might ask, "Why is Janie mean to the girls at the playground? Do you think that's nice?" Always followed of course with, "I know I can depend on you to be kind."

These conversations can be about TV shows, or even games the children play. The key at this age is constant conversation, at mealtime, in the car, while shopping, or in a waiting room, always reminding children that their first conclusion—about anything—may need to be reassessed.

Continue the Conversation

Certainly continue the conversation about friends and neighbors as the kids grow up, but expand it too. Is there a tax referendum for the public schools in your town? Ask older kids if they think taxpayers should pay more for public education. Your children may say "No" because, after all, your family does not even use the schools, so you get no benefit. Not entirely true; your house is worth more if you live in a school district with a good reputation. Will spending more money help to ensure that? Are the funds they have now being used wisely? Ask your children to research the issue.

As you can see, the possibilities are endless. As this book is being written, several candidates are running for the presidency who have little or no political experience. Should they be considered as serious candidates? Perhaps the learning curve will be too great for them to be effective leaders. On the other hand, our nation was founded by private citizens who wished to serve, not career politicians. Which way should voters turn? Perhaps your family will lean towards the citizen statesman, but then become concerned when inexperience seems to lead to less than savvy remarks. Maybe the non-politician will promise to appoint experienced department secretaries and advisors. Should voters insist on this in advance? Is the nation better off with a Washington veteran? A presidential election is often a fine time to discuss how judgments can change over time.

Literary Analysis

This ability to test judgments will be refined as students begin to read, and especially as they work on book reports, which are the beginning of literary analysis. Let's consider the familiar main character in Charles Dickens's *A Christmas Carol*, Ebenezer Scrooge. Dickens introduces Scrooge as a "squeezing, wrenching, grasping, scraping, clutching, covetous old sinner," and gives ample evidence in the plot to confirm a reader's poor opinion of him.

Then as Scrooge examines his early life with the Ghost of Christmas Past, the reader gains some insight into his motivation and even some sympathy in consideration of his lonely childhood. At the end of the tale, his time with the spirits has transformed Scrooge into "as good a friend, as good a master, and as good a man, as the good old city knew."

Examples abound in high quality literature. The entire plot of Jane Austen's classic *Pride and Prejudice* centers on how preconceived notions affect our personal relationships, actions, and plans, but one needn't wait until high school. Fairy tales deal with this theme again and again. Snow White's evil stepmother is beautiful, often an indicator of goodness in fairy tales, but not in this case. She considers herself to be the most beautiful woman in the land, but being forced by the mirror to test this idea, leads to her great hatred of Snow White. Hansel and Gretel, left to starve in the woods, joyfully find a house made of gingerbread and candy in the woods, but soon realize that it is a trap set by a wicked witch who eats children. Initial judgments are often wrong.

This theme really concerns the necessity of keeping an open mind. People can change, or our opinions of them may change. Events may not be as they first seemed, and further study causes us to reassess our first opinion. Understanding that first impressions are frequently flawed, or that people and situations may change over time develops a proper sense of humility, and deep insight into the human condition, essential in a leader.

Conclusion

Elite private boarding schools were an important cornerstone in the foundation of a permanent American upper class whose children were to be socialized for power. They were great schools for the Great Race, intended to forge a collective identity among children of privilege, training them to be bankers, financiers, partners in law firms, corporate directors, negotiators of international treaties and contracts, patrons of the arts, philanthropists, directors of welfare organizations, members of advisory panels, government elites, and business elites.

John Taylor Gatto

Catholic Homeschooling – Our Best Hope

What is our take-away?

This book concerns, at its heart, the future leadership of America — our communities, our nation and our Church. Some of us may have children who, because of their abilities and ambitions, will excel at just about everything they undertake. The central thesis of this book is that we have an opportunity denied to the parents of children in the government school system. We can help — or perhaps serve as guides as they help themselves — to place our well-formed Catholic children in positions where they can exert a strong influence for good

Some may be thinking that their children, while precious, are more ordinary in both aptitude and aspiration. After decades of teaching in urban public schools, John Taylor Gatto observed that "genius is an exceedingly common human quality," and that "the unlikeliest kids kept demonstrating to me so many of the hallmarks of human excellence — insight, wisdom, justice, resourcefulness, courage, [and] originality." I suspect we will find these same qualities in the vast majority of our homeschooled children if we just look for them, but it really doesn't matter. It is no less important to prepare those who appear to be more ordinary for leadership because indeed they will be future leaders in their families, parishes, neighborhoods, and workplaces. They can be a powerful force for good at a local level, and their influence will transform communities for the better.

It is our solemn responsibility as parents/teachers to encourage all our children to develop strong character, diligent work habits, and highly trained intellects, always pointing them towards excellence.

The Path to Leadership

John Taylor Gatto advises us to get out of kids' way and give them space and time and respect. His writings wistfully recall a time when children ran free exploring their environment, and learned naturally and willingly because they saw the benefit of it in everyday life. In those early days before compulsory education, children frequently attended school sporadically or even barely at all. Yet he advises parents to, "Pick up a fifth-grade math or rhetoric textbook from 1850 and you'll see that texts were pitched then on what today would be considered college level." Is Gatto's approach, which seems to be geared towards what some call unschooling, the way to proceed?

Today's Challenges

Modern American society offers many challenges and obstacles to an "unschooling" vision of education.

- Decades ago, John Gatto spoke of television "mass commercial entertainment" as being "addictive as any other hallucinogenic drug." The situation has only worsened with the addition of the Internet and, most especially, video games. In too many families, including those who educate at home, the screens go on as soon as Mom's back is turned. Children are not exploring their world; they are escaping from it to an electronic universe, much of it utterly devoid of any value.

- Before electronic entertainment, families would converse during meals and read to one another after supper. Now all eyes are glued to screens.

- In times past, a child's work ethic was built long before he learned to read or write through his labor within his family. It is not a burden to memorize spelling words or multiplication tables when one is accustomed to hauling wood and water, mucking out stables, loading trucks, or even pumping gas and washing windshields as my brothers did. Now children are rarely required to do more than pick up their own toys and make their own beds. Many are not expected to do even that.

- During my own childhood, children were expected to perform what would now be considered adult activities at remarkably young ages. When my husband was eight years old, his conductor father would send him alone on a New York City subway from Brooklyn into Manhattan to pick up sheet music. When I started kindergarten shortly after my fifth birthday, my mom paid a neighborhood girl

25¢ per week to walk me to school. Knowing the way, I was expected to walk home myself. After a few weeks she figured she would save the quarter; I was on my own. Today many parents do not allow 5th graders to walk unaccompanied down a suburban street to the school bus stop.

- Products of institutional schools themselves, many 21st century parents struggle to properly discipline their children and doubt their ability to provide a top-flight education at home. I am convinced that "freestyle" parenting and homeschooling would not be a viable option for the majority of families. Frankly in many communities, including my own, parents would be reported to social services for allowing their children to do meaningful work or explore communities on their own.

1 2 3 Practical Path to Follow

This book advocates a combination approach.

First, parents need to restore order and discipline to their home in a simple, common sense way. Despite everything one hears today, it is really a natural straightforward process as proven by millennia of uneducated men and women who raised simply delightful, obedient, hardworking children without the dubious wisdom of modern psychology. Parents who feel they need some help to establish patterns of calm, confident discipline, may wish to look at my book *It Doesn't Have to Be This Way*. I also highly recommend resources from Dr. Ray Guarendi, and especially for parents of boys, the writings of James Stenson.

Second, we must provide our children with an orderly, rigorous Catholic education in our homes. Some of you may feel you can do this by "picking and choosing" materials, but after over twenty years of meeting and speaking with home schooling parents, I urge great caution in taking this approach. My experience tells me that the best academic results are achieved when parents choose a curriculum based on excellence.

In the interest of full disclosure, I am presently an employee of Seton Home Study School, an example of a curriculum based on excellence. My children were enrolled in the program for fourteen years before they hired me, and I presently help to home educate my grandchildren who are enrolled in Seton. Although I am a pretty resourceful person, there is no way I could have put together a program of this quality on my own, nor given myself a comparable support system.

Like what I suspect are most families, I stray off Seton's program here and there adding French, substituting instrumental lessons for their music books, and using community sports programs for gym. Parents who have their children enrolled in Catholic home study programs commonly enroll them in junior colleges for upper level math, science, or foreign language. Most of us enrich our curricula with travel and "homeschool days" hosted by zoos, museums, and cultural institutions. All of these can flesh out our home education, but there needs to be the strong foundation of a solid Catholic home education program first.

Third and finally, John Taylor Gatto has identified these fourteen themes of prestigious private prep schools and pointed out the extraordinary number of their graduates who go on to leadership roles in business, the professions, arts and government. Take them to heart and consider how you can give your own children the benefits of independence, responsibility, right judgment and the other virtues found in the chapters of this book. They are the ingredients for leadership

What will the world look like when our children are adults?

The stakes are high when we consider the influence intellectually prepared, virtuous men and women with impeccable character could wield in the future. It is our sacred responsibility to give homeschooled students a deep desire to serve both God and their fellow man, sanctifying their own lives and evangelizing others through their professional work, whatever that might be. Our nation, our Church, and our world need them. A future dominated by well-formed, deeply committed Catholic leaders is a lovely world to contemplate.

We Catholic homeschooling parents will one day stand before God and have to give an accounting of our stewardship of the precious lives He entrusted to us. We are given only one unique and unrepeatable opportunity to raise our children for His service.

May He give us the graces we need for this mighty task.

Notes

Notes

Notes

Notes

Notes

Notes

Notes

More Homeschooling Wisdom from Ginny Seuffert

Available through seton**books**.com

Ginny's Gems: 10 Essentials for Teaching Your Preschooler at Home

Study after study shows that homeschooled children receive an all-around better education. The one-on-one relationship between the starter student and the teaching parent leads to astonishing academic progress.

In this little book with big advice you will find:
- Essential Toddler Do's and Don'ts
- How to Stimulate Your Child's Unlimited Potential
- Looking Ahead to Kindergarten and Beyond
- How to Overcome Objections from Friends and Family

Ginny's Gems: Home Management Essentials: 10 Ways to Make Your Homeschooling Journey Simpler and More Effective

Popular speaker at Home School conferences, and home schooling mother of 12 children, Mrs. Virginia "Ginny" Seuffert, offers a straightforward, practical guide to managing your home and family life amidst the exciting challenges of home schooling your children.

Ginny delivers her practical advice in her natural no-nonsense, commonsense, and humorous manner. This great book is intentionally short so that every busy home schooling mother can benefit from reading it.

Turn the messiest, unorganized house into a tidy, cheerful home!

It Doesn't Have To Be This Way!

For years parents have listened to author, lecturer, and homeschool veteran, Ginny Seuffert pound home the notion that clear, confident, and consistent parenting is the key to successful homeschooling.

This little book is short, sweet, and to the point. It is chock-full of practical, commonsense advice that has worked successfully for generations of parents.